PROCRASTINATION
Preventing the Decay of Delay

W9-AYA-180

JUNE HUNT

HENDRICKSON PUBLISHERS   ROSE PUBLISHING

Procrastination: Preventing the Decay of Delay
Copyright © 2015 Hope For The Heart
Aspire Press is an imprint of
Rose Publishing, LLC
P.O. Box 3473
Peabody, Massachusetts 01961-3473 USA
www.hendricksonrose.com

Unless otherwise indicated, all Scripture quotations are from the THE HOLY BIBLE, NEW INTERNATIONAL VERSION®, NIV® Copyright © 1973, 1978, 1984, 2011 by Biblica, Inc.™ Used by permission. All rights reserved worldwide.

Scripture quotations marked "NKJV™" are taken from the New King James Version®. Copyright © 1982 by Thomas Nelson, Inc. Used by permission. All rights reserved.

Scripture quotations marked (NASB) are taken from the New American Standard Bible®, Copyright © 1960, 1962, 1963, 1968, 1971, 1972, 1973, 1975, 1977, 1995 by The Lockman Foundation. Used by permission. (www.Lockman.org)

Scripture quotations marked (NLT) are taken from the Holy Bible, New Living Translation, copyright, © 1996, 2004. Used by permission of Tyndale House Publishers, Inc., Wheaton, Illinois 60189. All rights reserved.

Scripture quotations marked "ESV™" are from The Holy Bible, English Standard Version™. Copyright ©2001 by Crossway Bibles, a division of Good News Publishers. Used by permission. All rights reserved.

The views and opinions expressed in this book are those of the author(s) and do not necessarily express the views of Rose Publishing, nor is this book intended to be a substitute for mental health treatment or professional counseling.

The information in this resource is intended as guidelines for healthy living. Please consult qualified medical, legal, pastoral, and psychological professionals regarding individual concerns.

For more information on Hope For The Heart, visit www.hopefortheheart.org or call 1-800-488-HOPE (4673).

Printed in the United States of America

December 2017, 5th printing

CONTENTS

Dear Friend,

Everyone procrastinates, just at different times, in different ways, and for different reasons. We all (including me) have delayed doing what needs to be done. Many personal illustrations come to my mind. Most are about me, but the one I'll tell you about involves my mother.

Late one afternoon, I arrived at my mother's home to take her with me to a dinner where I was to sing "The Battle Hymn of the Republic." Yet, when I walked through her door, I began to sense a *battle* ensuing within *my* spirit. Mother had not even begun to get ready. She was most apologetic and most sincere—as usual. But her apologies couldn't change the fact that she had lost a battle with her consuming enemy. Instead of being able to control procrastination, procrastination had control of her.

Forty-five minutes later, as we began to leave her bedroom, the phone rang. When she moved to answer the phone, I couldn't believe it! "Wait!" I said strongly. "Why are you answering the phone?" Puzzled at my question, she responded logically, "Because it's ringing."

Calmly, I presented my logic to her, "But if we had left on time, you wouldn't be here to answer the phone." She looked stunned. Her hand waited, paralyzed above the receiver. The phone kept ringing, but slowly she moved her hand away. "Well, no, I wouldn't be. I've just never thought about it that way." In that moment she experienced a clear-cut paradigm shift—a new way of looking at life—at least in regard to the telephone.

Just because a phone rings doesn't mean that answering it is the *right* thing to do. In fact, if you're already late or if that call would cause you to be late, most of the time, answering would be the wrong thing to do. What freedom we can have from the tyranny of the telephone and from the reign of procrastination in our lives! That evening, my mother received a touch of that freedom.

If you, too, find yourself needing a new way of looking at life—a new strategy to do battle with that persistent and perplexing enemy called "procrastination"—I sincerely pray that through the truths within these pages you will become equipped with a new, stronger battle plan that will guide you to the freedom you've been looking for.

Yours in the Lord's hope,

June Hunt

PROCRASTINATION
Preventing the Decay of Delay

"Late again! How did this happen? Why didn't I start earlier? What is the matter with me? The deadline has come and gone, and here I am again—feeling guilty, frustrated, and defeated!"

Procrastination is a thief, stealing our confidence and integrity and continually robbing us of hearing those wonderfully rewarding words, "Job well done! Thanks for doing this on time!" Of course, others are continually robbed by not receiving what they need from us when they need it.

The hope of our hearts is the even greater truth that the Lord is able and willing to show us how to stop this destructive decay of delay. He can teach us how to manage time so that we can be counted on to be a blessing to others.

In truth, we can enjoy the fruit of motivation rather than the frustration of procrastination. As faithful servants, we want the Lord to consider us diligent and devoted and not consumed by *delay*. Notice one of the ways Jesus motivates us to be "wise managers."

"Who then is the faithful and wise manager,
whom the master puts in charge
of his servants to give them their food
allowance at the proper time?
It will be good for that servant whom the
master finds doing so when he returns."
(Luke 12:42–43)

DEFINITIONS

Few procrastinate all of the time. However, most people have at least one "pocket of procrastination"—an area where doing what needs to be done is often delayed.

Amazingly, procrastinators are usually quite optimistic about their ability to complete a task and are quick with reassurances: "I have everything under control."

Temporarily lulled by a false sense of the time required, they lope along with an *unscheduled starting time* and an *undefined deadline*. Suddenly, as the time to finish rapidly approaches, their minds start reeling, *Oh no—I feel out of control! I've barely begun. How could this happen again?*

Actually, asking the question, "How could this happen?" is helpful because ...

"The wisdom of the prudent is to give thought to their ways,
but the folly of fools is deception."
(Proverbs 14:8)

The picture of procrastination can be clearly seen in a parable. Although the word *procrastination* itself is not found in Scripture, many characteristics, causes, and cures are in plain view throughout the Bible.

Jesus talks about the distribution of talents—silver monetary tokens given in various amounts to three different men based on their giftedness and abilities. One is given *five* talents, another *two*, and yet another only *one*. Their master then goes away on a journey. When he returns, he evaluates their results.

The man with five talents wastes no time putting his money to work, doubling his investment, which prompts praise from his master. The man with two talents does likewise, reaping two more along with his master's praise. But the man with the one talent lacks initiative and assumes no responsibility to invest his money. He merely digs a hole in the ground and fearfully hides his lone token, which results in an unexpected repercussion that reveals the servant's shortsightedness.

Jesus calls this servant lazy and adds this practical rebuke, *"You should have put my money on deposit with the bankers, so that when I returned I would have received it back with interest"* (Matthew 25:27).

The master proceeds to take away his talent and give it to the man with ten talents, the man who was not negligent, but diligent. Ultimately, Jesus applies the parable to the rewards of diligence and the lack thereof. Therefore, whatever God gives you the ability and responsibility to do, do it and you will find joy in your reward.

The Bible says ...

> "Whatever you do, whether in word or deed,
> do it all in the name of the Lord Jesus,
> giving thanks to God the Father
> through him."
> (Colossians 3:17)

▶ **Procrastinate** means to avoid or put off needlessly an action that needs to be taken.

"Sluggards [those who have a lifestyle of procrastinating] *do not plow in season; so at harvest time they look but find nothing"* (Proverbs 20:4).

▶ **Procrastination** is the habit of delaying what needs to be done, which results in both inner and outer repercussions.[1]

- *Inner repercussions* range from feeling discouraged and dejected to struggling with guilt, distress, and despair.

- *Outer repercussions* range from missed deadlines and missed appointments to lost employment and lost relationships.

"One who is slack in his work is brother to one who destroys" (Proverbs 18:9).

▶ **Procrastinators** are often pictured in Scripture as slothful, sluggish, and lazy. The Old Testament Hebrew word *atsel* means indolent, idle, or slack.[2]

"How long will you lie there, you sluggard? When will you get up from your sleep?" (Proverbs 6:9).

Procrastination vs. Laziness

QUESTION: "Is there a difference between procrastination and laziness?"

ANSWER: Many people assume that procrastinators are always lazy—however, laziness is just one cause of procrastination. If you are lazy, you are negligent in handling your responsibilities because of choosing not to do what you need to do.

On the other hand, you may be highly productive and in no way lazy, but still procrastinate by simply failing to start a task on time or not accurately predicting how long it will take. This procrastinator desires to work and yet delays, whereas the lazy procrastinator lacks desire and refuses to work. Proverbs, the book of wisdom, warns us about the way of the sluggard.

"The way of the sluggard
is blocked with thorns,
but the path of the upright is a highway."
(Proverbs 15:19)

Procrastinators who don't want to procrastinate typically do not understand themselves at all, especially when they repeatedly miss both self-imposed and other-imposed deadlines. Truth is, they feel like failures and browbeat themselves over their lack of discipline and irresponsibility in failing to meet time commitments. They procrastinate not by design, but by default.

On a continuum from mild to extreme, this negative pattern of behavior is an outgrowth of five "personality types." Unintentional procrastinators put off doing what should be done because of one or more of these five underlying roots: *perfectionism, poor self-worth, fear, lack of goals, and feeling overwhelmed.*

These unintentional procrastinators *want* to change but don't know *how* to change. They don't know why they do what they don't want to do, nor do they know how to begin doing what they do want to do. Eventually, wave after wave of hopelessness overtakes them. However, if they can gain wisdom about themselves and about God's will and His willingness to help them, not only can their lives be changed but their futures can also be full of hope.

"Know also that wisdom is like honey for you: If you find it, there is a future hope for you, and your hope will not be cut off."
(Proverbs 24:14)

#1 PERFECTIONIST PATTY

Overly consumed with what she does—not who she is—Patty feels paralyzed when she can't measure up to the unrealistic standards she sets for herself. She feels she must perform perfectly, yet finds herself stymied when she discovers that perfection is unattainable! With such a mind-set, who wouldn't suffer the paralysis of procrastination? Patty puts impossible expectations on herself, only to find that her self-worth suffers. Her "inner critic" is her constant companion.

- **Patty's Thinking**: Focused on "performance-based acceptance"

  "I must do this perfectly. Anything short of perfection is failure."

- **Patty's Feeling**: Critical of self and others; hardest on herself

  "If it's not perfect, I'll feel horrible."

- **Patty's Response**: Engages in self-deception; works hard; prerequisites must be in place

  "I can't start until I have everything just right."

- **Patty's Assumption**: Procrastinates because of not wanting to appear imperfect

  "If I do it perfectly, I'll be accepted. I won't be rejected."

Conclusion: Perfectionist Patty procrastinates because she is never satisfied with her performance. She doesn't realize that God doesn't demand perfection, but rather desires that she aim for excellence. Patty needs to be at peace in her times of stress and learn to rely on His strength. The Lord says ...

> "My grace is sufficient for you, for my power is made perfect in weakness."
> (2 Corinthians 12:9)

#2 Poor Self-Worth Paul

Overly controlled by what others think and because he views himself so poorly, Paul struggles just to get started. Since in his heart he doesn't feel acceptable, he assumes that nothing he does will be acceptable. Paul's negative self-talk makes any goal unattainable. He tends to think, *So why try?* When he makes mistakes, rather than learning lessons and persevering through to completion, his low self-worth weighs him down, and he simply gives up trying.

- **Paul's Thinking**: Dominated by early messages of inadequacy

  "I am such a failure. I can't do anything right!"

- **Paul's Feeling**: Inadequate and that he has no real value

  "I feel so insignificant, so incapable, so incompetent, so worthless!"

- **Paul's Response**: Compares himself to others, remains passive

  "I'm not good enough to succeed. There's no sense in trying."

- **Paul's Assumption**: Procrastinates because of feeling inferior

  "I'm sure I will fail."

Conclusion: Poor self-worth Paul procrastinates because he lacks God's perspective of his value. Paul can't see what he is capable of achieving. He doesn't realize that God not only created him, but also preplanned the work He designed Paul to do. The Bible says ...

> "We are God's handiwork, created in Christ Jesus to do good works, which God prepared in advance for us to do."
> (Ephesians 2:10)

#3 Fear-Based Freddie

Overly afraid of people and unknown circumstances, Freddie sees life as risky and sidesteps responsibility in order to feel safe. When faced with an assignment, he feels anxious. *What if I make a costly mistake?* Freddie's fear paralyzes him from following through with a task because he expects a negative reaction from others. Freddie's procrastination is *focused* not only on his own performance—which he perceives as flawed—but also on the opinions of others, which he fully expects to be condemning.

- **Freddie's Thinking**: Clouded by imagined concerns; a classic worrier

  "I know I won't succeed, and that will be horrible!"

- **Freddie's Feeling**: Afraid of confrontation, his fear of conflict takes control.

  "I dread starting something that might go wrong and cause conflict."

- **Freddie's Response**: Puts off anything that could evoke a negative reaction

  "I'm afraid to start because I'm sure to fail."

- **Freddie's Assumption**: Procrastinates because of fear of conflict

  "If I put it off, I won't have to deal with it."

Conclusion: Fear-based Freddie procrastinates because he believes any effort has the potential of initiating a rejection—if not an explosion! Freddie doesn't have to be controlled by fear because even in stressful situations he can claim ...

> "In God I trust and am not afraid.
> What can man do to me?"
> (Psalm 56:11)

#4 LACK-OF-GOALS LARRY

Overly dependent on others for decision making, Larry has no real sense of purpose for his life. He hopes that one day his life will amount to something. But because Larry has no clear direction, he has difficulty setting goals, making decisions, and staying focused. His lack of purpose makes beginning any task a burden.

- **Larry's Thinking**: Scattered and confused like a ship without a rudder; can't steer because he has no map

  "I don't know why I am doing what I'm doing."

- **Larry's Feeling**: Lost because he doesn't know where he's going

  "No matter what I do, I don't feel fulfilled."

- **Larry's Response**: Knows he needs to chart the course, but finds himself dead in the water

  "Why start this task when it really doesn't make any difference?"

- **Larry's Assumption**: Procrastinates because he has no direction

  "I need to wait until I can figure out what I really want to do."

Conclusion: Lack-of-goals Larry delays accomplishing tasks because he is unable to see how any of his efforts contribute to a meaningful goal. Larry doesn't realize that God has planned a fulfilling course for him. The Bible says ...

"Our people must learn to devote themselves to doing what is good, in order to provide for urgent needs and not live unproductive lives."
(Titus 3:14)

#5 Overwhelmed Olivia

Overly committed to being a people pleaser, Olivia's work area looks like a disaster zone. Her phone is likely lost under a stack of "to-do" lists. Someone is coming by in five minutes, but she is already 10 minutes late for another meeting. Olivia works feverishly, but finds no way to get on top of it all. There just isn't enough time in the day for her to do what she needs to do.

- **Olivia's Thinking**: Overcome with overload

  "I'm doing the best I can, but there's no way I can finish on time."

- **Olivia's Feeling**: Ill-equipped for handling tasks

  "My life feels out of control."

- **Olivia's Response**: Chooses easiest tasks first over the most important

  "Since I can't get it all done on time, I'll work on a project that I really enjoy and at least accomplish something."

- **Olivia's Assumption**: Procrastinates because of being on overload.

  "I just need to work harder and faster somehow."

Conclusion: Overwhelmed Olivia procrastinates because she feels responsible for more than she can handle, yet has no ability to manage her time in a meaningful way. Olivia doesn't realize that she has all the time she truly needs because God will never require more of her than she can do.

Olivia needs to take this verse to heart ...

"The wise heart will know the proper time and procedure. For there is a proper time and procedure for every matter."
(Ecclesiastes 8:5–6)

Procrastinating vs. Postponing

QUESTION: "Is it ever right to procrastinate intentionally and postpone working on a task?"

ANSWER: No, it's never right to procrastinate, but to postpone a task can be prudent. These are two different issues. Procrastination and postponement are not the same. You may have legitimate reasons for postponing a task.

For rational reasons, you need to postpone or even not do a task when ...

> ▸ It isn't your highest priority.

> ▸ It will keep you from a previous commitment.

> ▸ It will compromise your health.

> ▸ It appears urgent, but it isn't important.

> ▸ It is important, but it is not your task to complete.

> ▸ It is you who should do it, but beginning it now would be premature.

Be aware that doing a task could be *right*, but the timing could be *wrong*. Proverbs 19:2 says, *"Desire without knowledge is not good—how much more will hasty feet miss the way!"*

2 Confused

- They legitimately choose to avoid action because of a lack of clarity or a misunderstanding of what to do and how to do it.

- Rather than barge ahead without wisdom, their confusion leads them to not act.

The Bible declares, *"If any of you lacks wisdom, you should ask God, who gives generously to all without finding fault, and it will be given to you"* (James 1:5).

3 Controlling

- They choose to avoid action through passive-aggressive tactics in order to control or irritate others indirectly.

- Rather than prioritizing what needs to be done, they prioritize their personal agendas.

In contrast, the Bible says, *"Do nothing out of selfish ambition or vain conceit"* (Philippians 2:3).

4 Lazy

- They choose to avoid action because of apathy, self-centeredness, or a poor work ethic.

- Rather than develop discipline to do the undesirable, they do only what they want to do, what they "feel" like doing.

The Bible gives this graphic description: *"Through laziness, the rafters sag; because of idle hands, the house leaks"* (Ecclesiastes 10:18).

5 REBELLIOUS

- They choose to avoid action as a means of defying authority.

- Rather than submit to authority, they set themselves up as their own authorities.

"There are those who rebel against the light, who do not know its ways or stay in its paths" (Job 24:13).

Joshua and Caleb vs. the Ten Faithless Spies

Imagine being an Israelite under the leadership of Moses. You've seen it all:

▷ God supernaturally saves all the Israelites from Egyptian slavery. (Ten catastrophic plagues pressure Pharaoh to allow them to leave.)

▷ God supernaturally parts the Red Sea and more than 2,000,000 Israelites walk on dry ground to the other side.

▷ God supernaturally closes the Red Sea so that the entire Egyptian army in hot pursuit drowns as walls of water fall on them.

Now God has given this specific directive ...

" ... go up to the land I promised. ... I will send an angel before you and drive out the [enemies]. ... Go up to the land flowing with milk and honey." (Exodus 33:1–3)

After seeing Almighty God supernaturally provide manna and quail for all the Israelites and even witnessing Him pour water out of a rock, would you really hesitate to obey Him? Still, Moses sends twelve spies to scout out the land God had promised them. But when they return with their reports, ten scouts adamantly say *they must not go*! In doing so, their fear-based procrastination causes years of needless wandering and waiting in reaching their Promised Land.

Procrastination vs. Waiting on God

QUESTION: "What is the difference between waiting on God and procrastinating?"

ANSWER: Procrastinating is knowing what action you need to take but then failing to take it. Waiting on God occurs after taking the needed action of seeking God for direction, inquiring of Him as to what you need to do next in a particular situation.

▶ You cannot do what you do not yet know to do.

▶ You should not do what you know to do until you know when, where, and how to do it.

While waiting for God to reveal what He wants you to do, everything you know to do is to be done without hesitation.

▶ When we do what God has already made clear and take the steps He has shown us, He will reveal the "next step" in His perfect timing.

▶ As the saying goes, "God unrolls His scroll one line at a time."

It may also be that you need to wait on God to make a decision simply because you are in a state of grieving the loss of someone or something significant to you.

▶ Those grieving a significant loss are not able to sufficiently focus mentally or emotionally in order to make sound, life-changing decisions.

▶ The best course of action in such a case is to take no action but to wait until you have gone through the grieving process for one to four years before tackling difficult decisions. The Bible makes it clear that we are to depend on God to direct our paths and the steps we take.

"Trust in the LORD with all your heart
and lean not on your own understanding;
in all your ways submit to him,
and he will make your paths straight. ...
A person's steps are directed by the Lord.
How then can anyone understand
their own way?"
(Proverbs 3:5–6; 20:24)

Creation clearly demonstrates God's work ethic and the diligent work ethic He designed for us. For six days He labored and on the seventh day, after completing His work, He rested, but not before then. Likewise, He charged the first man and woman to work in the garden He created. Genesis 2:15 says, *"The LORD God took the man and put him in the Garden of Eden to work it and take care of it"* (Genesis 2:15).

Later, we discover how the sons of Adam and Eve also worked diligently: *"Now Abel kept flocks, and Cain worked the soil"* (Genesis 4:2). Then God made the work ethic the law of the land.

> "Six days you shall labor and do all your
> work, but the seventh day is
> a sabbath to the LORD your God."
> (Exodus 20:9–10)

God's Heart Regarding Diligence

God's heart on procrastination is revealed throughout the Bible by addressing both the negligent and the diligent. In the Bible as a whole, God's heart regarding diligence is disclosed. In Proverbs the negligent and the diligent are contrasted. And in the Epistles, Christians are exhorted to work diligently.

▶ **God's heart** is that we work diligently, because diligence produces progress.

"Be diligent in these matters; give yourself wholly to them, so that everyone may see your progress" (1 Timothy 4:15).

▶ **God's heart** is that we be diligent to fulfill the promises we make to Him.

"When you make a promise to God, don't delay in following through, for God takes no pleasure in fools. Keep all the promises you make to him" (Ecclesiastes 5:4 NLT).

▶ **God's heart** is that we diligently encourage each other to do loving acts and good works for others.

"Let us think of ways to motivate one another to acts of love and good works" (Hebrews 10:24 NLT).

▶ **God's heart** is that we diligently do the works of God while we can.

"As long as it is day, we must do the works of him who sent me. Night is coming, when no one can work" (John 9:4).

▶ **God's heart** is that we be diligent in finishing the work God gives us to do.

"I have brought you glory on earth by finishing the work you gave me to do" (John 17:4).

▶ **The negligent** are never filled but the diligent are fully filled.

"A sluggard's appetite is never filled, but the desires of the diligent are fully satisfied" (Proverbs 13:4).

▶ **The negligent** have a blocked way but the diligent travel the highway.

"The way of the sluggard is blocked with thorns, but the path of the upright is a highway" (Proverbs 15:19).

▶ **The negligent** focus on fantasies but the diligent focus on work.

"Those who work their land will have abundant food, but those who chase fantasies have no sense" (Proverbs 12:11).

▶ **The negligent** experience poverty but the diligent experience profit.

"All hard work brings a profit, but mere talk leads only to poverty" (Proverbs 14:23).

▶ **The negligent** are filled with poverty but the diligent are filled with food.

"Those who work their land will have abundant food, but those who chase fantasies will have their fill of poverty" (Proverbs 28:19).

▶ **Diligently work** to share with others.

"Anyone who has been stealing must steal no longer, but must work, doing something useful with their own hands, that they may have something to share with those in need" (Ephesians 4:28).

▶ **Diligently work** for the Lord, not others.

"Whatever you do, work at it with all your heart, as working for the Lord, not for human masters, since you know that you will receive an inheritance from the Lord as a reward. It is the Lord Christ you are serving" (Colossians 3:23–24).

▶ **Diligently work** to not be a burden to others.

"Surely you remember, brothers and sisters, our toil and hardship; we worked night and day in order not to be a burden to anyone while we preached the gospel of God to you" (1 Thessalonians 2:9).

▶ **Diligently work** with your hands.

"Make it your ambition to lead a quiet life: You should mind your own business and work with your hands, just as we told you" (1 Thessalonians 4:11).

▶ **Diligently work** or you won't eat.

"For even when we were with you, we gave you this rule: 'The one who is unwilling to work shall not eat'" (2 Thessalonians 3:10).

CHARACTERISTICS OF UNINTENTIONAL PROCRASTINATORS

Procrastinators wear multiple faces. Although unintentional procrastinators can be put into one of five groups, identifying which group a person fits into is not always easy. Although someone can be a combination of several types, one "face" generally dominates.

To identify your prevailing type, evaluate your behavior, your motivation, and your internal dialogue or personal thoughts. Then make a commitment to face the truth about your procrastination. Follow up with a commitment to devise a plan that will help you persevere so that you can be the mature person God intends for you to be.

James 1:4 says ...

"Let perseverance finish its work so that you may be mature and complete, not lacking anything."

Checklist for Possible Procrastinators

Are you plagued with procrastination? The following questions will help you determine whether you have potholes of procrastination causing your life to be chaotic and disjointed. Place a (✓) check mark by each question that you answer with a *yes*.

☐ Do you delay starting projects?

☐ Do you collect materials for projects but struggle to move forward?

☐ Do you hinder the efforts of others by delaying your part?

☐ Do you deliberately work slowly or inefficiently?

☐ Do you resent suggestions on how to be more productive?

☐ Do you avoid competition and other situations where you might not succeed?

☐ Do you act indecisively and force others to make decisions?

☐ Do you shirk responsibility by focusing on the faults of others?

☐ Do you dodge making or keeping commitments?

☐ Do you become irritable when asked to do something unpleasant?

☐ Do you find yourself consistently late for appointments?

- ❏ Do you neglect obligations by supposedly "forgetting" them?
- ☐ Do you pay bills and other financial obligations late?
- ☐ Do you fail to return phone calls?
- ☐ Do you postpone sending correspondence until it is too late?
- ☐ Do you live in a state of disorganization?
- ☐ Do you become addicted to time-wasting activities (for example, TV, shopping, computer games, social media)?
- ☐ Do you feel "spiritually bankrupt," yet reject the Bible's riches?
- ☐ Do you desperately need direction, yet fail to pray for God's guidance?
- ☐ Do you resist God's correction by rejecting His conviction?

As you ask yourself these questions, realize ...

"The heart of the discerning
acquires knowledge,
for the ears of the wise seek it out."
(Proverbs 18:15)

Deeply involved in a mental game of self-deception, procrastinators remain hopeful and avoid admitting anything is wrong. They convince themselves that they will do the unpleasant task *tomorrow*, thus denying that they are even procrastinating. The "tomorrow principle" is unending and skillfully perpetuated by self-talk that rationalizes and rearranges priorities. The only problem with this tactic is, *tomorrow is never today*!

As the Bible says ...

> "I applied my heart to what I observed and learned a lesson from what I saw."
> (Proverbs 24:32)

1 PERFECTIONIST PATTY

Patty is a hard worker, but she's hardest on herself. Deeply involved in a mental game of self-deception, this perfectionist thrives on performance-based acceptance: *I must perform perfectly or I won't be accepted.* A litany of prerequisites must be in place before tackling a task or bringing any project to completion.

- "This must be perfect. I'll start when I have a large block of time."

- "I must wait until I know I can do a first-class job."

- "I can't make the deadline. I'll extend it in order to do it right!"

- "Regardless of what I promised, I can't turn this in. It may have mistakes."

- "I don't know if I really did my best. I need to do it again."

The Bible describes the necessity of finishing our work, not just wanting it finished: *"Now finish doing it also, so that just as there was the readiness to desire it, so there may be also the completion of it by your ability"* (2 Corinthians 8:11 NASB).

2 POOR SELF-WORTH PAUL

Paul goes through life worried about what others think about him. Always comparing himself to others, he secretly feels he has no real value. Paul would love to do something important, but his feelings of inferiority cause him to be passive and to procrastinate. He delays getting important things done.

- "Why should I start? I can't do it."

- "There's no sense in trying; it never will be good enough."

- "What I do won't make any difference."

- "I don't have anything of value to contribute."

- "I don't have what it takes to succeed."

Worry becomes destructive when it is constant and keeps God's truth from bearing fruit in our lives.

"The worries of this life, the deceitfulness of wealth and the desires for other things come in and choke the word, making it unfruitful" (Mark 4:19).

3   FEAR-BASED FREDDIE

Freddie is the classic worrier. He goes through life being afraid of any kind of confrontation. Fear of conflict takes control of his life—fear of criticism, anger, and rejection. Rather than face negative responses, he puts off anything that could evoke a reaction. Meanwhile, his fear-based thinking only produces more and more procrastination.

- "If I make a decision, I'm afraid it will be rejected."

- "I don't want to work on this now and look bad in front of others."

- "I'm afraid they'll get mad at me, so I'll deal with it tomorrow."

- "I don't want to do this; I'll just get criticized again."

- "I'm afraid for others to see my work. They won't think it's good enough."

The Bible gives this warning about fear . . .

"Fear of man will prove to be a snare, but whoever trusts in the LORD is kept safe" (Proverbs 29:25).

4 LACK-OF-GOALS LARRY

Larry is like a ship without a rudder—he can't stay on course. He has no map and no clue about where he's heading. He sees others setting goals and achieving them, but Larry doesn't have any direction for himself. He knows he needs to chart the course, but instead finds himself dead in the water.

- "I feel like I'm stuck—I'm not going anywhere."

- "I really don't know what to do."

- "I don't even know what I want."

- "I don't know how to get started."

- "I feel like I'm going in the wrong direction."

Larry needs to learn to draw from his talents and abilities in order to set achievable goals so progress can be made and revealed.

"Each of you should use whatever gift you have received to serve others, as faithful stewards of God's grace in its various forms" (1 Peter 4:10).

5 OVERWHELMED OLIVIA

Olivia is overcome with overload. She has not learned the skill of handling tasks on time; therefore, she lives each day in a sea of distress. Until she learns how to prioritize, she will be overcome by conflicting tasks, lack of focus, urgent demands, and the needs of others. To reduce the pile imprisoning her, she selects the easiest task first rather than the one that's most important. She starts one task after another, but fails to finish most of them on time.

- "I can't get anything done because of all the phone calls and interruptions."

- "I have so many deadlines that I don't know where to start."

- "These assignments are too hard for me."

- "I can't handle this workload."

- "I don't like to tell anyone 'No.'"

If you fail to allow the Lord to initiate your plans, you will find that your own plans will fail.

"If their purpose or activity is of human origin, it will fail" (Acts 5:38).

CAUSES OF PROCRASTINATION

The influence of our early family relationships runs deep. Harmful words heard as a child about *who you are* and *what you do* can handicap your heart for a lifetime.

If you have a problem with procrastination, begin looking for answers by writing down the messages you received in childhood—from your parents and other important people in your life.

Then, write the assumptions you took to heart that may still be influencing your behavior today—especially since the Bible says ...

> "The tongue has the power
> of life and death."
> (Proverbs 18:21)

Imagine: After a painful fall, your body lies paralyzed. You are rushed to the doctor. Immediate action is needed to reverse the condition. Today, many people could be diagnosed with a malady called the "paralysis of procrastination." It begins in childhood as a result of injurious words, yet those grown children put off getting the help they so desperately need to reverse their condition.

Sadly, most who suffer from this condition did not contract it quickly and neither do they heal *quickly*. They meet and plan, set goals and deadlines, schedule and reschedule, but the problem goes far beyond a daily regimen for good time management. Beneath the surface are wrong beliefs that keep procrastinators paralyzed.

To discover God's prescription for healing, procrastinators need large doses of God's Word, of God's truth—their thinking needs to line up with God's thinking because ...

"He sent out his word and healed them."
(Psalm 107:20)

PERFECTIONIST PATTY

Children yearn for love, praise, and acceptance. If they don't feel valued for *who they are*, but only for *what they do*, they believe that performing perfectly is the one way to gain approval.

Patty's Perceived Messages

- "If it's not done right, it's not worth doing at all." "It's vital that I be the best." "I'm not as good as my brother—I have to do better."

Patty's Assumption

- "If it's not perfect, it's not acceptable."

The Result for Patty

- A *perfectionistic* personality

Patty's Problem

- Since no one does everything perfectly, perfectionists often procrastinate in order to prevent even the possibility of imperfection.

Biblical Perspective for Patty

"I am the vine; you are the branches. If you remain in me and I in you, you will bear much fruit; apart from me you can do nothing " (John 15:5).

Those with low self-worth were often given messages of inadequacy, insignificance, and failure for what they did or didn't do during their younger years. In their hearts, their small, childhood failures have been interpreted to mean they have no worth and nothing of value to contribute. This inner message can remain with them for a lifetime.

Paul's Perceived Messages

- "I'm so stupid." "I can't do anything right." "I'll never amount to anything."

Paul's Assumption

- "I'm worthless and will never be good at anything, so why try?"

The Result for Paul

- A *poor self-worth* personality

Paul's Problem

- Paul does not realize that he has been created with value and worth; therefore, the lies he tells himself encourage him to procrastinate to avoid revealing his perceived inadequacy.

Biblical Perspective for Paul

"Are not five sparrows sold for two pennies? Yet not one of them is forgotten by God. Indeed, the very hairs of your head are all numbered. Don't be afraid; you are worth more than many sparrows" (Luke 12:6–7).

Fear-Based Freddie

Children long for closeness and want to feel safe and secure with both their mother and father. But when a child's offer of love is rejected—and they are treated harshly—they become fearful and believe that people cannot be trusted. This belief often continues into adulthood.

Freddie's Perceived Messages

- "If I don't please my parents, they won't love me." "I want to run away and hide when my mother gets angry." "If my dad doesn't like what I do, he'll take it out on mom and me."

Freddie's Assumption

- "If I fail and make someone angry, the consequence will be terrible."

The Result for Freddie

- A *fear-based* personality

Freddie's Problem

- Freddie's fear of harsh judgment affects his confidence and his trust in others. This debilitating fear causes him to use procrastination as a means of avoiding people and responsibilities.

Biblical Perspective for Freddie

"God hath not given us the spirit of fear; but of power, and of love, and of a sound mind" (2 Timothy 1:7 KJV).

Many people, confused about what is important to them, were children and adolescents whose authority figures—namely parents—made most of the decisions for them. As a result, they failed to develop healthy independence and became too dependent on others for decision making. Now, as adults, their confusion leads to greater indecision about the direction of their lives. Just as you cannot walk to a destination if you don't know where it is, you cannot achieve goals if you don't know what they are.

Larry's Perceived Messages

- "I'm not able to make my own decisions." "If I don't like this class, I can get out of it." "If I get caught in a jam, my parents will smooth it out."

Larry's Assumption

- "I don't know what my purpose in life is. I can't make decisions by myself."

The Result for Larry

- A *lack-of-goals* personality

Larry's Problem

- Since Larry has never had to establish and stick to goals, he procrastinates because he has no clear focus or direction.

Biblical Perspective for Larry

"All hard work brings a profit, but mere talk leads only to poverty" (Proverbs 14:23).

5 OVERWHELMED OLIVIA

Some people never learn the word *no* as children and as a result are conditioned to be "people pleasers." Whenever others invade their schedule and eat up their time, they don't realize that they can set personal boundaries. Even though they love being everyone's "savior," such a position of responsibility has become too difficult to maintain in adulthood.

Olivia's Perceived Messages

- "The more I do, the more I'll be liked." "If I do a lot of projects, my parents will be proud of me." "I can't say *no* to others. I'm responsible for making them happy."

Olivia's Assumption

- "I'm the solution to everyone's problems. It feels good to have a lot to do, but it feels bad to disappoint people when I have so much to do that I fail to get it all done."

The Result for Olivia

- An *overwhelmed* personality

Olivia's Problem

- Because Olivia's responsibilities have become so overwhelming, she doesn't know where to start and finds herself gravitating toward easier tasks. Rather than give more important tasks top priority in her schedule, she takes on unimportant tasks first.

Biblical Perspective for Olivia

"What you are doing is not good. ... The work is too heavy for you; you cannot handle it alone" (Exodus 18:17–18).

Combined Causes

QUESTION: "Could I have a combination of causes for procrastination?"

ANSWER: Yes. One person could be both a *perfectionist* and *overwhelmed*, resulting in a major struggle with procrastination. Another person could delay needlessly because of both *low self-worth* and a *lack of goals*. Whether your procrastination stems from one cause or several, each and every temptation to procrastinate can be overcome.

The Bible says ...

"Watch and pray so that you will not fall into temptation. The spirit is willing, but the flesh is weak."
(Matthew 26:41)

Olivia sits staring at the mounds of paper on her desk. When Larry walks up and asks, "Do you have an idea for your story yet?" Olivia replies, "I'm waiting for inspiration." Then she dramatically exclaims, "You just can't turn on creativity like a faucet. You have to be in the right mood!" Larry asks, "What mood is that?" Olivia casually replies, "Last-minute panic."

In her heart, Olivia wants to get things done on time and without panic, but every time a deadline draws near, she's behind and frantic. We, like Olivia, don't have to be motivated by a state of panic, yet too often we let a last-minute crisis derail our good intentions. Regretfully, we share the sentiment stated in this verse: *"I do not understand what I do. For what I want to do I do not do, but what I hate I do"* (Romans 7:15).

Four Contributing Factors to Needless Delay

▶ **Learned behavior**. Over time, we generally learn how to respond in life by observing and "copying" those around us. We also form our own opinions about what behaviors work for us.

- This means you can *unintentionally learn* a pattern of procrastination when you follow the example of significant people in your life and subconsciously model yourself after those who needlessly delay doing what needs to be done.

- This also means you can *intentionally unlearn* a pattern of procrastination by determining to learn new behaviors and by modeling yourself after responsible, productive adults who do not delay doing what needs to be done.

"Let the wise listen and add to their learning, and let the discerning get guidance" (Proverbs 1:5).

▶ **Lack of self-discipline.** A lack of organizational skills is more of a *technique problem*, whereas a lack of self-discipline is more of an *emotional problem*. (For example, feelings of fear, inadequacy, and low self-worth are all emotional problems that can cause you to delay doing what needs to be done.)

- This means your emotional needs can override your pressing need to be productive. When this happens, your emotional problems have prevented you from practicing self-discipline.

- This also means you can choose to free yourself from debilitating emotional needs by developing a plan to have those needs met legitimately. (You can also elicit the help of wise, mature Christians as you become emotionally healthy and learn organizational skills.)

"The Lord will guide you always; he will satisfy your needs in a sun-scorched land and will strengthen your frame" (Isaiah 58:11).

▶ **Poor project management.** Feeling overwhelmed by the enormity of a large task is often the result of seeing it as one huge job rather than a complex project with several smaller, more manageable components.

- This means you believe that something must be done perfectly the first time and that there is no room for trial and error.

- This also means you can choose to address the underlying causes that led you to become a perfectionist and then accept the truth that you must not demand perfection from yourself or others (an expectation that is unrealistic). Rather, you can choose to aim for excellence.

"How much better to get wisdom than gold, to get insight rather than silver!" (Proverbs 16:16).

▷ **Poor time management.** Not using time wisely when working on a project can lead to disaster.

- This means you incorrectly estimate the time necessary for the completion of a task or you fail to allocate sufficient time in your schedule for a given task.

- This also means you can learn to discern the order in which tasks need to be accomplished and then block out the time required for each task. Most importantly, you can also learn to stick to your plan! (You can seek help from good time managers to estimate realistically the time needed to perform specific tasks. Then you can add extra "pad time" to allow for unexpected interruptions.)

"Let us discern for ourselves what is right; let us learn together what is good" (Job 34:4).

Every person has three inner needs: the needs for love, significance, and security.[3] Because these God-given needs are always present, procrastination can become a protective strategy to avoid negative responses from others.

Procrastinators can hide behind excuses, such as, "If I delay doing *it* (whatever needs to be done), I won't be rejected, I won't feel inadequate, and I won't be a failure. I just haven't gotten around to *it*."

They tenaciously hold to a self-critical way of thinking that makes starting and finishing their top priorities very difficult.

Their wrong beliefs keep them stuck in a cycle of fear, frustration, and failure!

The Bible says ...

> "Folly brings joy to one who has no sense,
> but whoever has understanding
> keeps a straight course."
> (Proverbs 15:21)

Three God-Given Inner Needs

▶ **Love**—to know that someone is unconditionally committed to our best interest

"My command is this: Love each other as I have loved you" (John 15:12).

▶ **Significance**—to know that our lives have meaning and purpose

"I cry out to God Most High, to God who fulfills his purpose for me" (Psalm 57:2 ESV).

▶ **Security**—to feel accepted and a sense of belonging

"Whoever fears the LORD
has a secure fortress, and for their
children it will be a refuge."
(Proverbs 14:26)

The Ultimate Need-Meeter

Why did God give us these deep inner needs, knowing that people fail people and self-effort fails us as well?

God gave us these inner needs so that we would come to know Him as our Need-Meeter. Our needs are designed by God to draw us into a deeper dependence on Christ. God did not create any person or position or any amount of power or possessions to meet the deepest needs in our lives. If a person or thing *could* meet all our needs, we wouldn't need God! The Lord will use circumstances and bring positive people into our lives as an extension of His care and compassion, but ultimately only God can satisfy all the needs of our hearts. The Bible says ...

> "The Lord will guide you always;
> he will satisfy your needs in a sun-scorched
> land and will strengthen your frame.
> You will be like a well-watered garden,
> like a spring whose waters never fail."
> (Isaiah 58:11)

The apostle Paul revealed this truth by first asking, *"What a wretched man I am! Who will rescue me from this body that is subject to death?"* and then by answering his own question in saying it is *"Jesus Christ our Lord!"* (Romans 7:24–25).

All along, the Lord planned to meet our deepest needs for ...

▶ **Love**—*"I* [the Lord] *have loved you with an everlasting love; I have drawn you with unfailing kindness"* (Jeremiah 31:3).

▶ **Significance**—*"'For I know the plans I have for you,' declares the Lord, 'plans to prosper you and not to harm you, plans to give you hope and a future'"* (Jeremiah 29:11).

▶ **Security**—*"The Lord himself goes before you and will be with you; he will never leave you nor forsake you. Do not be afraid; do not be discouraged"* (Deuteronomy 31:8).

The truth is that our God-given needs for love, significance, and security can be legitimately met in Christ Jesus! Philippians 4:19 makes it plain:

"My God will meet all your needs according to the riches of his glory in Christ Jesus."

▶ **Wrong Beliefs**

- **The need for love**

  "I can't start this now because the only way I will be deserving of love is if I do it perfectly."

- **The need for significance**

  "If I first do what is easiest, even though it isn't most important, I can accomplish something *now*—then I'll feel better about myself."

- **The need for security**

  "It's safer to delay than to take a risk and fail."

Right Belief

"My procrastination produces only guilt and a sense of incompetence and makes me feel like a failure. My deepest inner needs are met only by giving Christ control of my life. He will give me His power to overcome my procrastination and to develop His discipline in me."

"Not that we are competent in ourselves to claim anything for ourselves, but our competence comes from God."
(2 Corinthians 3:5)

The most costly procrastination is delaying the decision to receive Jesus Christ as your personal Lord and Savior. Many people rationalize, *I'm not ready. There's plenty of time. I'll do it one day—someday—another day.* However, that day may never come! Meanwhile, the Bible says ...

" ... now is the day of salvation."
(2 Corinthians 6:2)

Do You Want to Stop Delaying?

If so, realize ...

THE FOUR POINTS OF GOD'S PLAN

#1 God's Purpose for You is *Salvation.*

What was God's motivation in sending Jesus Christ to earth?

To express His love for you by saving you!

The Bible says, *"God so loved the world that he gave his one and only Son, that whoever believes in him shall not perish but have eternal life. For God did not send his Son into the world to condemn the world, but to save the world through him"* (John 3:16–17).

What was Jesus' purpose in coming to earth?

To forgive your sins, to empower you to have victory over sin, and to enable you to live a fulfilled life!

Jesus said, *"I have come that they may have life, and that they may have it more abundantly"* (John 10:10 NKJV).

#2 Your Problem is *Sin.*

What exactly is sin?

Sin is living independently of God's standard—knowing what is right, but choosing what is wrong.

The Bible says, *"If anyone, then, knows the good they ought to do and doesn't do it, it is sin for them"* (James 4:17).

What is the major consequence of sin?

Spiritual death, eternal separation from God.

Scripture states, *"Your iniquities* [sins] *have separated you from your God"* (Isaiah 59:2).

"The wages of sin is death, but the gift of God is eternal life in Christ Jesus our Lord" (Romans 6:23).

#3 God's Provision for You is the *Savior.*

Can anything remove the penalty for sin?

Yes! Jesus died on the cross to personally pay the penalty for your sins.

The Bible says, *"God demonstrates his own love for us in this: While we were still sinners, Christ died for us"* (Romans 5:8).

Belief in (entrusting your life to) Jesus Christ as the only way to God the Father.

Jesus says, *"I am the way and the truth and the life. No one comes to the Father except through me"* (John 14:6).

"Believe in the Lord Jesus, and you will be saved" (Acts 16:31).

#4 Your Part is *Surrender.*

Give Christ control of your life, entrusting yourself to Him.

"Jesus said to his disciples, 'Whoever wants to be my disciple must deny themselves and take up their cross [die to your own self-rule] *and follow me. For whoever wants to save their life will lose it, but whoever loses their life for me will find it. What good will it be for someone to gain the whole world, yet forfeit their soul?'"* (Matthew 16:24–26).

Place your faith in (rely on) Jesus Christ as your personal Lord and Savior and reject your "good works" as a means of earning God's approval.

"It is by grace you have been saved, through faith— and this is not from yourselves, it is the gift of God—not by works, so that no one can boast" (Ephesians 2:8–9).

The moment you choose to receive Jesus as your Lord and Savior—entrusting your life to Him—He comes to live inside you. Then He gives you His power to live the fulfilled life God has planned for you. If you want to be fully forgiven by God and become the person God created you to be, you can tell Him in a simple, heartfelt prayer like this:

PRAYER OF SALVATION

"God, I want a real relationship with You.
I admit that many times I've chosen to go
my own way instead of Your way.
Please forgive me for my sins.
Jesus, thank You for dying on the cross to
pay the penalty for my sins.
Come into my life to be my Lord
and my Savior.
Change me from the inside out
and make me the person
You created me to be.
In Your holy name I pray. Amen."

WHAT CAN YOU NOW EXPECT?

If you sincerely prayed this prayer, know that from this day forward, as you submit yourself to Him, the Lord will help you overcome procrastination.

"You [the LORD] make known to me
the path of life; you will fill me with joy
in your presence, with eternal pleasures
at your right hand."
(Psalm 16:11)

STEPS TO SOLUTION

Regardless of the cause of procrastination, whether it is rooted in childhood or not, people who consistently procrastinate demonstrate an irresponsible lack of concern for their own personal obligations and for the feelings and responsibilities of others.

The Bible says ...

> "Let each of you look not only
> to his own interests,
> but also to the interests of others."
> (Philippians 2:4 ESV)

Key Verses to Memorize

According to Scripture, to procrastinate is to put off doing that which is needful when there is no legitimate reason to do so—this debilitating behavior is not wise but unwise! Not only does it show disregard for those who are adversely impacted by it, to procrastinate fails to make the most of God's gift of opportunities for you.

For the Procrastinator

> "Be very careful, then, how you live—
> not as unwise but as wise,
> making the most of every opportunity."
> (Ephesians 5:15–16)

For the Motivator

Key Passages to Read

Many valuable lessons for living can be learned from observing the world around us and those living in that world, both the wise and the unwise.

For the Procrastinator

"I went past the field of a sluggard, past the vineyard of someone who has no sense; thorns had come up everywhere, the ground was covered with weeds, and the stone wall was in ruins. I applied my heart to what I observed and learned a lesson from what I saw: A little sleep, a little slumber, a little folding of the hands to rest—and poverty will come on you like a thief and scarcity like an armed man."
(Proverbs 24:30–34)

Parable of the Procrastinator

What can you observe about unmotivated procrastinators?

▶ They have a God-given opportunity to be productive.

"*I went past the field of a sluggard* [procrastinator], (v. 30)

▶ They lack good sense.

"*past the vineyard of someone who has no sense*; (v. 30)

▶ Everything around them is out of control.

"*thorns had come up everywhere,* (v. 31)

▶ They are negligent about their responsibilities.

"*the ground was covered with weeds,* (v. 31)

▶ Over time, their procrastination leads to ruin.

"*and the stone wall was in ruins.* (v. 31)

▶ We have something to learn by observing procrastinators.

"*I applied my heart to what I observed and learned a lesson from what I saw*: (v. 32)

▶ They justify their procrastination by minimizing its seriousness.

"*A little sleep, a little slumber, a little folding of the hands to rest—* (v. 33)

▶ They wake up with nothing and feel that they have been robbed!

"*and poverty will come on you like a thief and scarcity like an armed man.*" (v. 34)

For the Motivator

JOHN 13:1–16:11

What can we do in helping others overcome their inclinations to procrastinate? How can we best help prevent their needless "decay of delay"? Some use fear tactics, but fear of painful repercussions can further paralyze a procrastinator. Others use rewards, but rewards can be viewed as bribes. In truth, the greatest motivator in the world is love. Grasping the truth that we are unconditionally loved can help us all overcome our propensities to procrastinate and can motivate us to do what we need to do when we need to do it. Since God plans to accomplish His plan through us ...

> " ... let us not love with words or speech but with actions and in truth."
> (1 John 3:18)

HOW DOES JESUS MOTIVATE HIS DISCIPLES?

John's Gospel, chapters 13–16, records the final words of Jesus to His disciples—words so motivating that they have watered the growth of Christians for almost 2,000 years.

▶ **Jesus motivates** with a relationship of love. (**John chapter 13**)

- He loves completely. (13:1)

- He serves humbly. (13:2–17)

- He inspires love toward others. (13:31–34)

- He demonstrates faithfulness in the face of unfaithfulness. (13:38)

▶ **Jesus motivates** with rewards.
(**John chapter 14**)

- He promises heaven. (14:1–7)

- He promises the Holy Spirit. (14:15–26)

- He promises peace. (14:27)

- He promises joy after suffering. (16:22)

▶ **Jesus motivates** with repercussions.
(**John chapter 15**)

- He explains God's discipline. (15:1–2)

- He explains the consequences of failing to remain dependent on Him. (15:5–8)

- He explains the reason that the world sins against Him. (15:18–16:4)

- He explains the judgment resulting from this sin. (16:5–11)

Jesus uses all three methods of motivation: repercussion, reward, and relationship; however, the most mature method is a *relationship of unfailing love*. Jesus is our model for motivating others with a steady stream of *agape* love (always seeking the highest good of others). His love moves people to action. Ultimately, Jesus motivates and inspires those who know Him to be all God created them to be.

▶ **Diligently work** to share with others.

"Anyone who has been stealing must steal no longer, but must work, doing something useful with their own hands, that they may have something to share with those in need" (Ephesians 4:28).

▶ **Diligently work** for the Lord, not others.

"Whatever you do, work at it with all your heart, as working for the Lord, not for human masters, since you know that you will receive an inheritance from the Lord as a reward. It is the Lord Christ you are serving" (Colossians 3:23–24).

▶ **Diligently work** to not be a burden to others.

"Surely you remember, brothers and sisters, our toil and hardship; we worked night and day in order not to be a burden to anyone while we preached the gospel of God to you" (1 Thessalonians 2:9).

▶ **Diligently work** with your hands.

"Make it your ambition to lead a quiet life: You should mind your own business and work with your hands, just as we told you" (1 Thessalonians 4:11).

▶ **Diligently work** or you won't eat.

"For even when we were with you, we gave you this rule: 'The one who is unwilling to work shall not eat'" (2 Thessalonians 3:10).

▶ **The negligent** are never filled but the diligent are fully filled.

"A sluggard's appetite is never filled, but the desires of the diligent are fully satisfied" (Proverbs 13:4).

▶ **The negligent** have a blocked way but the diligent travel the highway.

"The way of the sluggard is blocked with thorns, but the path of the upright is a highway" (Proverbs 15:19).

▶ **The negligent** focus on fantasies but the diligent focus on work.

"Those who work their land will have abundant food, but those who chase fantasies have no sense" (Proverbs 12:11).

▶ **The negligent** experience poverty but the diligent experience profit.

"All hard work brings a profit, but mere talk leads only to poverty" (Proverbs 14:23).

▶ **The negligent** are filled with poverty but the diligent are filled with food.

"Those who work their land will have abundant food, but those who chase fantasies will have their fill of poverty" (Proverbs 28:19).

When I know what I should do yet can't seem to do it, I need to "prevent the decay of delay" by spending time alone and reflecting over two or three occasions in the past when I needlessly put something off. Then I will write down what I remember.

▶ What responsibility did I put off?

▶ What led me to procrastinate?

▶ What feelings did I have?

▶ What was the outcome of my procrastination?

▶ What other people were affected by my lack of follow-through?

▶ Were there any common patterns of behavior? For example, was I afraid of someone's response? Am I "fear-based"?

While this awareness alone will not bring about change, it can motivate me to take the following ten steps.

"Instruct the wise and they will be wiser still; teach the righteous and they will add to their learning."
(Proverbs 9:9)

1 **Acknowledge** that procrastination smothers all sense of motivation.

   "The craving of a sluggard [procrastinator] *will be the death of him, because his hands refuse to work"* (Proverbs 21:25).

2 **Tell** God that I am tired of fighting the clock. Pray for wisdom and help in using the time He has given me.

   "There is a proper time and procedure for every matter ... " (Ecclesiastes 8:6).

3 **Keep** a record at all times, tracking everything I need to do and checking off each task with the exact day and time I complete it.

   " ... there will be a time for every activity, a time to judge every deed" (Ecclesiastes 3:17).

4 **Refuse** to "major on the minors" but keep the "main thing" the "main thing" by prioritizing each day the five most important tasks to be done. Then do them in that order.

   " ... he who follows empty pursuits will have poverty in plenty" (Proverbs 28:19 NASB).

5 **Estimate** the time needed to complete each project—be realistic. Then add additional time for "hidden costs": unexpected interruptions, reviews, and delays.

"Suppose one of you wants to build a tower. Won't you first sit down and estimate the cost to see if you have enough money to complete it? For if you lay the foundation and are not able to finish it, everyone who sees it will ridicule you" (Luke 14:28–29).

6 **Resist** the temptation to feel guilty if an unforeseen situation arises making it impossible for me to complete all my tasks in one day. Continue to persevere to the next day, again giving top priority to the five most important tasks.

"Do not throw away your confidence; it will be richly rewarded. You need to persevere so that when you have done the will of God, you will receive what he has promised" (Hebrews 10:35–36).

7 **Consider** the impact of my negative self-talk when I get emotionally stuck. Change my thoughts and internal dialogue to reflect God's truth about me and to please God.

"May these words of my mouth and the meditation of my heart be pleasing in your sight, LORD, my Rock and my Redeemer" (Psalm 19:14).

8 **Ask** a friend or someone wise to help me if I struggle with getting started.

"The way of fools seems right to them, but the wise listen to advice" (Proverbs 12:15).

9 **Yield** my life to Christ, giving Him total control.

"I have been crucified with Christ and I no longer live, but Christ lives in me. The life I now live in the body, I live by faith in the Son of God, who loved me and gave himself for me" (Galatians 2:20).

10 **Claim** God's promise to provide everything I need through my dependence on Christ.

"His divine power has given us everything we need for a godly life through our knowledge of him who called us by his own glory and goodness. Through these he has given us his very great and precious promises, so that through them you may participate in the divine nature, having escaped the corruption in the world caused by evil desires" (2 Peter 1:3–4).

HOW TO Break the Power of Procrastination

Overcome the destructive power of procrastination in your life by tapping into encouraging affirmation and motivation. Then gain momentum as you move into *action*! You no longer have to live with discouragement or defeat, tied up with tension, riddled with remorse, and controlled by impossible ideals or feelings of fear or inadequacy.

Liberation definitely is within your reach. To be set free requires taking a long look at your past in order to understand *how* you became a prisoner of procrastination and *why* you have remained a prisoner for so long.

Liberation also requires that you identify all of the "mind games" you have played with yourself and others—the excuses or rationalizations that have *enabled* you to justify your procrastination. Once you take responsibility for these rationalizations and replace them with truth, you will have mastery over them. And once you are no longer a prisoner of the past, you will no longer be a perpetual *procrastinator*!

"'I have the right to do anything,' you say—
but not everything is beneficial.
'I have the right to do anything'—but I will
not be mastered by anything."
(1 Corinthians 6:12)

Those who seek perfection actually live in a world full of imperfect tension. Contrary to what most perfectionists secretly think, their quest for perfection is not something to be admired. Perfectionism is, in fact, a fault. Patty finds delegation especially difficult because perfectionists have a preference for doing their work themselves. They think, *If I do it, it'll be "done right."* How can Patty begin to avoid the trap of "doing things just right" and move toward the goal of just doing the right thing? The first step is to master your mind.

> "Do not conform to the pattern of this world, but be transformed by the renewing of your mind. Then you will be able to test and approve what God's will is—his good, pleasing and perfect will."
> (Romans 12:2)

Eight Cs to Control Your Thoughts

1. **Commit** to asking God to make you aware of your excessive demands and to enable you to let Him take charge of your thoughts each day.

   "Lord, prick my conscience whenever I demand perfection of myself or others."

2. **Confess** and eliminate your "all-or-nothing" thinking.

   "Lord, I admit that I've thought, *If it's not perfect, it's not worth doing.* I know that's wrong."

3. **Catch** yourself when you are being critical of others by overgeneralizing.

   "Lord, if I'm upset with someone and I start to say, 'You never … !' or 'You always … !' convict me in my spirit."

4. **Correct** any unrealistic expectations of yourself and others.

   "Lord, I'm putting away the *should*s, *ought-to*s, *must*s, and *have-to*s that I've tragically imposed on others and myself."

5. **Cease** all personal comparisons with others.

   "Lord, when someone does something better than I do, I know I don't have to feel awful!"

6. **Cancel** your rigid, personal rules.

   "Lord, I see that I don't have to be perfect to prove that I'm not a failure."

7. **Choose** to be satisfied with "less-than-perfect" work.

   "Lord, thank You that I need not *demand perfection*, but rather *aim for excellence*."

8. **Conquer** negative thoughts about yourself by replacing them with positive truths from God's Word.

   "Lord, thank You that Jesus '*saved us, not because of righteous things we had done, but because of his mercy*'" (Titus 3:5).

I affirm that ...

1 "**No one is perfect.** Flawlessness is a foolish goal."

   "There is no one righteous, not even one" (Romans 3:10).

2 "**I never have to fear losing God's love**, no matter how I perform."

   "I am convinced that neither death nor life ... nor anything else in all creation, will be able to separate us from the love of God that is in Christ Jesus our Lord" (Romans 8:38–39).

3 "**I will not live as a prisoner** of my past."

   "Forget the former things; do not dwell on the past. See, I am doing a new thing! Now it springs up; do you not perceive it? I am making a way in the wilderness and streams in the wasteland" (Isaiah 43:18–19).

4 "**I will not fear condemnation**, even when I fail to meet the expectations of others."

   "There is now no condemnation for those who are in Christ Jesus" (Romans 8:1).

5 "**I will stop comparing myself** with others."

   "We do not dare to classify or compare ourselves with some who commend themselves. When they measure themselves by themselves and compare themselves with themselves, they are not wise" (2 Corinthians 10:12).

6 "**I will take on new challenges** with confidence—I don't have to be perfect. I'm not limited to only the areas where I know I'll excel."

   "The LORD will be at your side and will keep your foot from being snared" (Proverbs 3:26).

7 "**I will not be anxious** about doing my work perfectly, but I will entrust everything in my life to the Lord. I can trust God to prepare the way for my future."

   "Do not be anxious about anything, but in every situation, by prayer and petition, with thanksgiving, present your requests to God" (Philippians 4:6).

8 "**I am free to enjoy life.** Instead of being in bondage to unrealistic expectations, the Lord wants me to be set free."

   "If the Son sets you free, you will be free indeed" (John 8:36).

Your worth is determined by God alone. God-given worth is unconditional. No hard words or harsh treatment can diminish your worth. No personal failure or weakness can threaten your worth. Yet, poor self-worth Paul lets the ups and downs of his daily life and the opinions of others determine how he feels about himself.

In truth, your sense of value, like poor self-worth Paul's, should not be based on rejection from others or on anything you have done or will do. Instead, your true worth must be secured in your belief that your intrinsic value comes from God's unchanging love and acceptance.

"The God and Father of our Lord Jesus Christ ... has blessed us with every spiritual blessing in the heavenly places in Christ, just as He chose us in Him before the foundation of the world, that we should be holy and without blame before Him in love, having predestined us to adoption as sons by Jesus Christ to Himself, according to the good pleasure of His will, to the praise of the glory of His grace, by which He made us accepted in the Beloved."
(Ephesians 1:3–6 NKJV)

1. **I accept** the fact that I was created in the image of God.

   "God created mankind in his own image, in the image of God he created them; male and female he created them" (Genesis 1:27).

2. **I accept** myself as acceptable to God.

   "May the God who gives endurance and encouragement give you the same attitude of mind toward each other that Christ Jesus had" (Romans 15:5).

3. **I accept** what I cannot change about myself.

   "Who are you, a human being, to talk back to God? 'Shall what is formed say to the one who formed it, "Why did you make me like this?"' Does not the potter have the right to make out of the same lump of clay some pottery for special purposes and some for common use?" (Romans 9:20–21).

4. **I accept** the fact that I will make mistakes.

   "Not that I [the apostle Paul] *... have already arrived at my goal, but ... Forgetting what is behind and straining toward what is ahead, I press on toward the goal* [Christlikeness] *to win the prize for which God has called me heavenward in Christ Jesus"* (Philippians 3:12–14).

5   **I accept** criticism and responsibility when I fail.

"I acknowledged my sin to you and did not cover up my iniquity. I said, 'I will confess my transgressions to the LORD.' And you forgave the guilt of my sin" (Psalm 32:5).

6   **I accept** the fact that I will not be liked or loved by everyone.

"If the world hates you, keep in mind that it hated me first. ... If they persecuted me, they will persecute you also" (John 15:18, 20).

7   **I accept** the unchangeable circumstances in my life.

"We know that in all things God works for the good of those who love him, who have been called according to his purpose" (Romans 8:28).

Seven Rebuttals to Self-Defeating Statements

1   If you say: "I don't have the strength to do what is right."

THE LORD SAYS: I'll give you My strength to do what is right.

"I can do all things through Christ who strengthens me" (Philippians 4:13 NKJV).

2   If you say: "I can't trust anyone."

THE LORD SAYS: I'll give you strength to trust Me.

"The LORD is my strength and my shield; my heart trusts in him, and he helps me. My heart leaps for joy, and with my song I praise him" (Psalm 28:7).

3 If you say: "I can't measure up."

THE LORD SAYS: I am able to help you measure up.

"God is able to bless you abundantly, so that in all things at all times, having all that you need, you will abound in every good work" (2 Corinthians 9:8).

4 If you say: "I don't feel that anyone loves me."

THE LORD SAYS: I love you.

"I have loved you with an everlasting love; I have drawn you with unfailing kindness" (Jeremiah 31:3).

5 If you say: "I can't forgive myself."

THE LORD SAYS: I will forgive you.

"If we confess our sins, he is faithful and just and will forgive us our sins and purify us from all unrighteousness" (1 John 1:9).

6 If you say: "I wish I'd never been born."

THE LORD SAYS: Before you were born, I had plans for you.

"Before I formed you in the womb I knew you, before you were born I set you apart" (Jeremiah 1:5).

7 If you say: "I feel that my future is hopeless."

THE LORD SAYS: The future I have for you is full of hope.

"'For I know the plans I have for you,' declares the LORD, 'plans to prosper you and not to harm you, plans to give you hope and a future'" (Jeremiah 29:11).

Fear-Based Freddie

As long as Freddie denies his deeply-rooted fear that someday someone will discover his flaws, he will not be able to connect with others on an intimate level. This fear prevents him from developing the courage to be honest with himself and with others. This fear also stands as a barrier to feeling and embracing the unconditional love of God.

If Freddie would allow himself to surface the buried pain in his past and begin to heal from the wounds of his childhood by lining up his thinking with God's thinking, he would be released to experience true freedom. Instead of being enslaved to debilitating dread, joy-filled optimism would empower him to accomplish his tasks on time.

"It is for freedom that Christ has set us free. Stand firm, then, and do not let yourselves be burdened again by a yoke of slavery." (Galatians 5:1)

1 **Can I train** my mind to control my anxiety? Yes!

The Bible says, *"Do not be anxious about anything, but in every situation, by prayer and petition, with thanksgiving, present your requests to God. And the peace of God, which transcends all understanding, will guard your hearts and your minds in Christ Jesus. Finally, brothers and sisters, whatever is true, whatever is noble, whatever is right, whatever is pure, whatever is lovely, whatever is admirable—if anything is excellent or praiseworthy—think about such things"* (Philippians 4:6–8).

2 **Is being delivered** from all the fears I've had for years really possible? Yes!

The Bible says, *"I sought the Lord, and he answered me; he delivered me from all my fears"* (Psalm 34:4).

3 **Why should I** not live in fear of anyone?

"The Lord is my light and my salvation—whom shall I fear? The Lord is the stronghold of my life—of whom shall I be afraid?" (Psalm 27:1).

4 **What should I** do to overcome my anxiety?

"Humble yourselves, therefore, under God's mighty hand, that he may lift you up in due time. Cast all your anxiety on him because he cares for you" (1 Peter 5:6–7).

5 **What assurance** do I have from God when I need peace and strength?

"The LORD gives strength to his people; the LORD blesses his people with peace" (Psalm 29:11).

6 **How can I** guard my heart and my mind when I have no peace?

The Lord takes this role upon Himself, according to the prophet Isaiah, who said, *"You will keep in perfect peace those whose minds are steadfast, because they trust in you"* (Isaiah 26:3).

SIX FEARS TO REPLACE WITH FACT AND FAITH

1 **FEAR:** "I can't help this feeling of intense fear!"

FACT: This feeling of fear is a bluff to my mind and body. It is not grounded in truth.

FAITH: *"Though an army besiege me, my heart will not fear; though war break out against me, even then will I be confident"* (Psalm 27:3).

2 **FEAR:** "I'm afraid I won't please others."

FACT: My peace comes, not from pleasing others, but from pleasing God.

FAITH: *"We make it our goal to please him, whether we are at home in the body or away from it"* (2 Corinthians 5:9).

3 **FEAR:** "I feel hopeless—I'm afraid I'll never change."

FACT: Nothing is hopeless. The Bible says that when I am in Christ, I am a new person, and He will continue to change me.

FAITH: *"If anyone is in Christ, the new creation has come: The old has gone, the new is here!"* (2 Corinthians 5:17).

4 **FEAR:** "My heart has so much fear that my mind can't think clearly."

FACT: God will guard my heart and mind and give me peace.

FAITH: *"The peace of God, which transcends all understanding, will guard your hearts and your minds in Christ Jesus"* (Philippians 4:7).

5 **FEAR:** "To be safe, I have to be in control and guard every step I take."

FACT: God is in control of my life, and He is with me step-by-step.

FAITH: *"In their hearts humans plan their course, but the LORD establishes their steps"* (Proverbs 16:9).

6 **FEAR:** "I feel trapped with no way of escape."

FACT: God always makes a way of escape.

FAITH: *"No temptation has overtaken you except what is common to mankind. And God is faithful; he will not let you be tempted beyond what you can bear. But when you are tempted, he will also provide a way out so that you can endure it"* (1 Corinthians 10:13).

Larry's life is going nowhere because he has no blueprint to guide him. His road map to success begins by seeking God's clearly defined purpose and goals for his life. Only then will he be able to take pride in what God desires to accomplish through him on the highway to a healthy God-given self!

As you seek the Lord to reveal the skills and talents He has chosen just for you, He will also give you confirmation along the journey that you are on His pathway. Seek God's will for your life by praying ...

> "Give your servant a discerning heart."
> (1 Kings 3:9)

Purposes vs. Goals

Purposes are different from goals; however, they are related. Your purpose answers the question, "Why am I here on earth?" Your goals answer the question, "What am I here on earth to do?" The relationship between the two is that the goals you set should work together to help you reach your purposes.

Purposes:

▶ Define the *reason* for your life.

- Purposes relate to the long-term plan God designed for you.

"In him we were also chosen, having been predestined according to the plan of him who

works out everything in conformity with the purpose of his will" (Ephesians 1:11).

▷ Establish God's target.

- Purposes are the inspiration behind your achievements.

"... continue to work out your salvation with fear and trembling" (Philippians 2:12).

▷ Explain the "why" of your life. (why you are here on earth)

- Purposes relate to the aim of your life.

"For those God foreknew he also predestined to be conformed to the image of his Son" (Romans 8:29).

▷ Develop your life message.

- Purpose produces inner peace.

"May the God of hope fill you with all joy and peace as you trust in him, so that you may overflow with hope by the power of the Holy Spirit" (Romans 15:13).

Goals:

▷ Define the *routes* to reach your purpose.

- Goals relate to the different types of work God leads you to do in order to accomplish your purpose.

"There are different kinds of service, but the same Lord. There are different kinds of working, but in all of them and in everyone it is the same God at work" (1 Corinthians 12:5–6).

▶ Explain the "what" of your life. (what you do on earth)

- Goals relate to the activities in your life.

"Be very careful, then, how you live—not as unwise but as wise, making the most of every opportunity... Therefore do not be foolish, but understand what the Lord's will is" (Ephesians 5:15–17).

▶ Measure the movements to the target.

- Goals are your individual achievements.

"And with you, Lord, is unfailing love'; and, 'You reward everyone according to what they have done'" (Psalm 62:12).

▶ Draw from your talents and abilities.

- Goals reveal outer progress.

"Each of you should use whatever gift you have received to serve others, as faithful stewards of God's grace in its various forms. If anyone speaks, they should do so as one who speaks the very words of God. If anyone serves, they should do so with the strength God provides" (1 Peter 4:10–11).

DEFINE YOUR LIFE PURPOSES AND GOALS

▶ **Discover your life purposes.**

- **Realize** that God has promised to reveal His purpose for your life.

"I will instruct you and teach you in the way you should go; I will counsel you with my loving eye on you" (Psalm 32:8).

- **Realize** the power of prayer to reveal God's purpose.

"The prayer of a righteous person is powerful and effective" (James 5:16).

- **Realize** that God will use your spiritual gifts to accomplish His purpose.

"We have different gifts, according to the grace given to each of us. If your gift is prophesying, then prophesy in accordance with your faith; if it is serving, then serve; if it is teaching, then teach; if it is to encourage, then give encouragement; if it is giving, then give generously; if it is to lead, do it diligently; if it is to show mercy, do it cheerfully" (Romans 12:6–8).

- **Realize** the value of asking practical questions.

What are my God-given responsibilities?

What activities have brought the greatest joy to my heart?

What work has been most successful for me?

What is my predominant, God-given spiritual gift?

What are my primary passions and desires?

"Take delight in the LORD, and he will give you the desires of your heart" (Psalm 37:4).

▷ **Develop a written purpose statement.**

- One purpose in my life is [to use the teaching gift God has given me to impact the lives of others].

- One purpose in my life is [to be the best parent I can be].

- My highest purpose is [for my life to be conformed to the character of Christ].

  Every Christian is *"predestined to be conformed to the image of his Son"* (Romans 8:29).

▷ **Determine the goals needed to accomplish the life purposes you've identified.**

- Goals should be *beneficial* and *important*.

  "I want a college education because it will enable me to become a teacher."

- Goals should be *reasonable* and *reachable*.

  "I would love to be a professional ball player, but my gifts are in teaching."

- Goals should be *specific* and *measurable*.

  "I plan to enter college after I work for two years to earn my tuition."

- Goals should be *controllable* and *not dependent on others*.

  "There's a bus route close to where I live in case I don't have transportation to get to college."

- Goals should *reinforce* your life purposes.

  "My plan is to attend seminars and lectures on preparing teaching plans and making classroom presentations in order to prepare myself for a teaching career."

- Goals should be *an extension of your values—* your commitment regarding right and wrong. (Values are your principles, convictions, ideals, and beliefs.)

- "I believe that teaching truth with integrity will be a means of accomplishing God's purpose for my life."

" ... the upright give thought to their ways."
(Proverbs 21:29)

Overwhelmed Olivia

For most people, more time is devoted to "working on the job" than to any other part of life. This simply means that implementing time management skills must be a high priority. However, because Olivia hasn't developed these skills or learned to delegate certain tasks to others, tension builds in her body and stress is high! God has much to say about using time wisely and even about finding satisfaction in our work. He certainly doesn't want us to live our lives in a straightjacket of stress.

"A person can do nothing better than to eat and drink and find satisfaction in their own toil. This too, I see, is from the hand of God."
(Ecclesiastes 2:24)

Subdivide a Large Project

▶ **Break** a large project down into smaller tasks.

▶ **Make** a list of the tasks within each subdivision of the larger project.

▶ **Prioritize** by numbering tasks in the order they should be accomplished.

▶ **Delegate** parts of the job that others can do— especially if the project is too big for one person to handle alone.

"The work is too heavy for you;
you cannot handle it alone.
... select capable men from all the people—
men who fear God, trustworthy men
who hate dishonest gain—
and appoint them as officials over
thousands, hundreds, fifties and tens. ...
That will make your load lighter,
because they will share it with you."
(Exodus 18:18, 21–22)

Prioritize Your Action Steps in Order to Achieve Your Goals.

Priorities help you know what you should do first.

▶ **Write** out your daily priorities and keep them visible.

▶ **Set** written deadlines for the completion of each priority.

▶ **Check** off tasks as they are accomplished.

▶ **Commit** to giving your goals top priority in your schedule.

▶ **Ask** yourself these questions:

- What are my goals?

- What activities do I need to plan in order to accomplish my goals?

- What priorities do I have to arrange?

- When do I plan to do each activity?

- How much time will each activity take?

- How much time should I allot for events that I cannot control?

> "The desires of the diligent
> are fully satisfied."
> (Proverbs 13:4)

PROFIT FROM TIME-SAVING TIPS

▶ **Create** a detailed filing system (one folder for each family member, appliance, warranty, etc.). Instead of allowing individual pieces of paper to "float," put each document in a designated folder in a filing cabinet for immediate recall.

▶ **Consider** color coding each category of files for easy identification: family and friends—orange, home—brown, finances—green, organizations—blue.

▶ **Use** a personal organizer and planner.

▶ **Keep** a pen and pad with you at all times. Write down every large and small task you need to do, no matter how small.

▶ **Give** top priority to the five most important projects. Then determine in what order those five projects need to be done.

▶ **Block out** certain days on your calendar for large projects and certain hours for smaller projects, then protect and use that allocated time for those scheduled projects.

▶ **Set** a deadline for the completion of each project. Realize that tasks usually expand to the time allotted for completion, whether long or short.

▶ **Move** a task that you're stuck on down the list, work on something else on your priority list, and then return to the original task.

  ▪ For even smaller tasks that continue to get overlooked, write each one on a list, cut the list into strips with one task on each strip, and place the strips into a bowl. When you have 15 or 20 minutes of free time, "go fishing!" Take one strip of paper out of your "fishbowl" and do the designated task immediately.

▶ **Group** all similar tasks together and do what is in that one group (for example, errands, shopping, repairs, house and yard work). Answer letters, calls, and e-mails in groups.

▶ **Schedule** appointments back-to-back while allowing adequate time to transition from one to the next.

▶ **Announce** the time you have available at the beginning of a conversation: "I only have about five minutes, but I wanted to talk with you about _____."

▶ **Stand up** when the time has come for someone to leave and say, "Thank you for coming. I appreciate what we've talked about."

▶ **Establish** concluding sentences for telephone conversations: "Before we hang up, I want to thank you for _____."

▶ **Evaluate** how many minutes you habitually run late (such as 15 minutes). Then add that time plus an additional five minutes to the time you would usually leave, thus allowing for last-minute interruptions and breaking the habit of tardiness.

▶ **Keep** your leaving time in mind and stick to it. If the time has come to leave or if you are even one minute late, don't answer the phone or do one more task (no matter how small). After all, if you had left on time, you wouldn't be there to do it.

"The plans of the diligent lead to profit."
(Proverbs 21:5)

Think of a time when you've fallen. You couldn't lift yourself up. You couldn't help yourself. You felt stuck! You needed an outstretched hand to help—someone special to lift you up. Procrastinators are tied to a habit that has them paralyzed, and they are blind to a solution. They need an "angel of mercy" to help motivate and bring insight and wisdom—a way out of their weary world.

▶ **Pray for the procrastinator.**

"Lord, I pray that (___name___) will be motivated to change from a pattern of procrastination and that through Your Spirit, permanent change will occur."

▶ **Propose an accountability plan.**

"If you like, I'm willing to help you devise a schedule that will help you accomplish your top priorities. Initially, as your accountability partner, I'd like for us to talk each day about your progress and to meet once a week."

▶ **Note the unmet needs.**

"God created you with three inner needs: for love, significance, and security.[4] Sometimes procrastination is a result of trying to fulfill unmet needs. When you procrastinate, do you identify with any of these scenarios?"

- Are you trying to meet your need for love by being a people pleaser? If so, you may have difficulty saying *no*; therefore, you may feel overwhelmed and find yourself procrastinating.

- Are you trying to meet your need for significance by making sure everything is perfect? If so, you may be procrastinating because you are afraid that you might fail once you begin a task.

- Are you trying to meet your need for security by not risking rejection? If so, you may be fearful that what you do may not be unacceptable to others, and this fear may lead you to procrastinate.

"Instead of relying on yourself to protect and meet your needs, rely on the Lord to guard your heart and fulfill your needs. Depend on Him to give you the strength and the discipline to do what you need to do when you need to do it."

▶ **Encourage the use of a daily calendar.**

"Buy a calendar with a 31-day log. Determine to use it daily to be the best steward of the time God has given you."

▶ **Properly order your priorities.**

"Write down all that you need to accomplish."

- Number these priorities in terms of their importance.

- Each day, work on only your five top priorities. Be certain to work on the top five in the order of their importance before you move on to other tasks on your list.

- Keep a list of other tasks that need to be done in the coming weeks or months after you've completed your current priorities.

▶ **Group similar goals.**

"Make separate lists for your calls, correspondence, errands, and chores. Then set aside at least one hour of each day on your calendar to do the most important tasks on each list (for example, Monday—calls; Tuesday—letters; Saturday—errands)."

▶ **Limit the number of options.**

"Don't give yourself too many options; if possible, only about three. Fewer choices mean faster decisions, and fewer choices also mean less second guessing (less changing your mind after a decision has been made)."

▶ **Compliment small accomplishments.**

"That's great. You are really making progress. I'm proud of you. I admire your diligence. Don't focus on what you haven't done—look at what you have done. I see that you are trying to be faithful to God by using your time wisely."

▶ **Use the sandwich method to confront failure.**

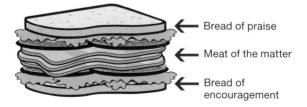

← Bread of praise

← Meat of the matter

← Bread of encouragement

- Bread of praise

  Mention a character trait: "I appreciate your perseverance. I see that you have really improved in this area. That's great!"

- Meat of the matter

  Be specific: "Why do you think you were late for (_____)? Are you aware that being late threw everyone else off schedule? What changes do you need to make so that you won't be late in the future?"

- Bread of encouragement

  Give hope: "I believe in you. I know you can do it."

▶ **Establish and maintain boundaries.**

"Because I will set aside time in my schedule to talk and meet with you, I will need you to be punctual and to keep our appointments. If you are late, we will have to wait until our next scheduled time to get together or to talk."

▶ **Set flexible, alterable arrangements.**

"If you are unable to keep some of our scheduled appointments, just give me a call a day or two before, and we will reschedule."

▶ **Acknowledge your own mistakes.**

"I can identify with your struggle. I remember when I was where you are now and how many times I fell back into my old patterns before I finally overcame them."

▶ **Avoid being manipulated into accepting another's responsibility.**

"I realize that you want me to do this for you, but doing this yourself is really important. I know that you are more than capable."

▶ **Present the ultimate purpose.**

"Do you know God's purpose for your life? God's purpose for every Christian is to be conformed to the character of Christ! Romans 8:29 says that you are *"predestined to be conformed to the image of his Son"*—that means you can have the discipline and self-control of Christ!"

Conclusion:

If you have a proclivity to procrastinate, then set your sights on a scriptural word picture: "running the race to win the prize." First Corinthians 9:24 says ...

"Do you not know that in a race all the runners run, but only one gets the prize? Run in such a way as to get the prize."

The prize is *mastering maturity*, which means being more and more conformed to the character of Christ. That means being all God created you to be and doing all God created you to do within the time constraints He has established. To "run the race" with confidence, you need to start and finish the race on time. Motivate yourself to get an extra push off the starting block by practicing this daily exercise.

Tell yourself the truth by rehearsing these three Rs:

▶ Reward

▶ Repercussion

▶ Relationship

> "By overcoming my pattern
> of procrastination,
> I will gain the *reward* of results,
> I will lose the *repercussion* of guilt,
> and I will better my *relationship*
> with God."
>
> —June Hunt

SCRIPTURES TO MEMORIZE

Does there have to be a **proper time and procedure** for everything as long as I get them done?

*"The wise heart will know the proper time and procedure. For there is a **proper time and procedure** for every matter."* (Ecclesiastes 8:5–6)

Did God create us to **do good works**?

*"We are God's handiwork, created in Christ Jesus to **do good works**, which God prepared in advance for us to do."* (Ephesians 2:10)

Why do I need to **persevere** in doing **the will of God**?

*"You need to **persevere** so that when you have done **the will of God**, you will receive what he has promised."* (Hebrews 10:36)

Why should I **work** hard to develop **perseverance**?

*"Let **perseverance** finish its **work** so that you may be mature and complete, not lacking anything."* (James 1:4)

How does a **wise** person deal with **opportunity**?

*"Be very careful, then, how you live— not as unwise but as **wise**, making the most of every **opportunity** ... "* (Ephesians 5:15–16)

How can I gain **wisdom** and avoid the **deception** of procrastination?

*"The **wisdom** of the prudent is to give thought to their ways, but the folly of fools is **deception**."* (Proverbs 14:8)

Is God able to **bless** me **abundantly** so that I will have **all** that I **need** to **abound in every good work**?

"God is able to bless you abundantly, so that in all things at all times, having all that you need, you will abound in every good work." (2 Corinthians 9:8)

If I'm a procrastinator and habitually **delay**, what should I tell myself?

"I will hasten and not delay … " (Psalm 119:60)

What will happen if I am **diligent** in fulfilling the **plans** God has for me?

"The plans of the diligent lead to profit." (Proverbs 21:5)

What will help me feel **fully satisfied** in my work?

"The desires of the diligent are fully satisfied." (Proverbs 13:4)

NOTES

1. Jane B. Burka and Lenora M. Yuen, *Procrastination: Why You Do It, What to Do About It* (Reading, MA: Addison-Wesley, 1983), 5.

2. James Strong, *Strong's Hebrew Lexicon*, electronic ed., Online Bible Millennium Ed. V. 1.13 (Timnathserah Inc., July 6, 2002)), H#6101.

3. Lawrence J. Crabb, Jr., *Understanding People: Deep Longings for Relationship*, Ministry Resources Library (Grand Rapids: Zondervan, 1987), 15–16; Robert S. McGee, *The Search for Significance*, 2nd ed. (Houston, TX: Rapha, 1990), 27–30.

4. Crabb, Jr., *Understanding People*, 15–16; McGee, *The Search for Significance*, 27–30.

HOPE FOR THE HEART TITLES

- *Adultery*
- *Aging Well*
- *Alcohol & Drug Abuse*
- *Anger*
- *Anorexia & Bulimia*
- *Boundaries*
- *Bullying*
- *Caregiving*
- *Chronic Illness & Disability*
- *Codependency*
- *Conflict Resolution*
- *Confrontation*
- *Considering Marriage*
- *Critical Spirit*
- *Decision Making*
- *Depression*
- *Domestic Violence*
- *Dysfunctional Family*
- *Envy & Jealousy*
- *Fear*
- *Financial Freedom*
- *Forgiveness*
- *Friendship*
- *Gambling*
- *Grief*
- *Guilt*
- *Hope*
- *Loneliness*
- *Manipulation*
- *Marriage*
- *Overeating*
- *Parenting*
- *Perfectionism*
- *Procrastination*
- *Reconciliation*
- *Rejection*
- *Self-Worth*
- *Sexual Integrity*
- *Singleness*
- *Spiritual Abuse*
- *Stress*
- *Success Through Failure*
- *Suicide Prevention*
- *Trials*
- *Verbal & Emotional Abuse*
- *Victimization*

www.hendricksonrose.com